Instructor's Manual

Basic
Economic
Principles

ROBERT A. LYNN   *University of Missouri*

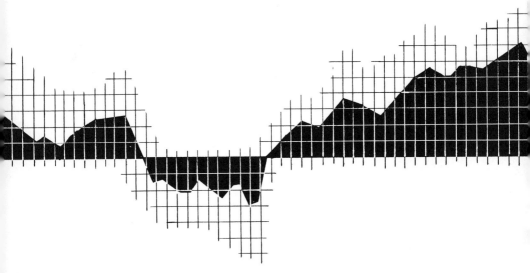

Instructor's Manual

Basic
Economic
Principles

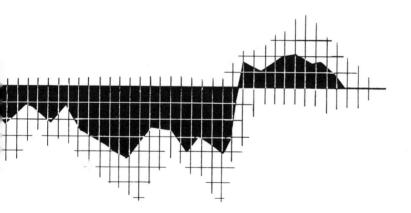

McGRAW-HILL BOOK COMPANY

New York • St. Louis • San Francisco

London • Toronto • Sydney

Instructor's Manual for BASIC ECONOMIC PRINCIPLES

39252

2 3 4 5 6 7 8 9 10 11 EBEB 7 5 4 3 2 1 0 6 9 8

PREFACE

Basic Economic Principles was written primarily as a text for a one-semester introductory course. Its scope of coverage and depth were planned with the goals of such a course in mind.

This manual is designed as an aid and guide to the instructors who will use the text. Many teachers will wish to use material of their own, perhaps quite different from that given here; others may use this manual only as an occasional reference. For those who desire it, however, full use of both the manual and the text should furnish a major basis for conducting the course.

There are two basic functions of class sessions. The first is to make sure that all necessary concepts and principles are understood by students. The second is to provide for a discussion of the significance and implications of the principles. There are many good methods of carrying out these functions. Those who follow this manual and the text closely will probably find themselves relying heavily on a question–answer and discussion approach. I would certainly not contend that this method is superior to any other. I can, however, assure users that I have tested it with students and found it thoroughly workable. The use of true-false questions, either turned in at once or self-graded, is especially appropriate for use before a chapter is discussed in class. They provide an incentive for study, they are reasonably simple, and they serve as springboards for both questions and discussions.

At the end of each chapter in the text is a group of questions called a ''Learning Key.'' This Key can be used most effectively if the student is encouraged to incorporate it in his study procedure. The following steps are recommended for using it most effectively.

1. Carefully read the summary at the end of the chapter.
2. Skim the chapter, examining the headings as well as the illustrations and their explanations.
3. Examine the questions in the Learning Key and try to formulate answers. (In most cases the student will probably not be able to give the correct answer, but exposure to the questions will give him an idea of what to look for as he reads the chapter. He can readily see if he is right by checking against the cue letters in the Key. These cue letters are either the first two letters of a word or the first letter of each word in a phrase.)
4. Read the assigned chapter, keeping in mind the questions found in the Learning Key.
5. Refer to the Learning Key again. This time the questions should be treated as an examination and the answers written on a sheet

of paper. The answers can be checked by referring to the Key. If the student does not recall the correct answer, he can turn to the page indicated at the end of the question and reread the section.

At the end of each part of the book, there is a compilation of the Learning Key questions from each chapter in that particular section. This Master Learning Key serves as an excellent review for examinations.

In writing Basic Economic Principles I have tried to guide myself by a realistic appraisal of what a student can be expected to comprehend from the maze of economics in a few months. I have also tried to bear in mind the special needs of the teacher who is not a specialist in this subject.

A major need in our times is the spreading of an understanding of economics. Such understanding is not beyond the comprehension of any alert citizen. The unique feature of economic news of the past few years is its increasing reflection of the work of modern economists. The educated citizen can no longer escape a confrontation with economic technicalities, if he wishes to be well informed. The purpose of the text and this manual is to provide a guide to a higher level of understanding.

Robert A. Lynn

CONTENTS

Chapter

PART I. ECONOMICS AND ECONOMIC INSTITUTIONS

CHAPTER 1

THE STUDY OF ECONOMICS

The outline used for this chapter will be repeated in all chapters. In addition to the reading references cited, there are many collections of readings which would be very useful. Examples include Readings in Current Economics (Revised) by Grossman, Hansen, Hendricksen, McAllister, Okuda, and Wolman (Richard D. Irwin, Homewood, Ill., 1961); Readings in Economics (3d ed.) by Samuelson, Bishop, and Coleman (McGraw-Hill, New York, 1958); and Selected Readings in Economics (2d ed.) by Clement L. Harriss (Prentice-Hall, Englewood Cliffs, N.J., 1962). Another useful reference source would be any of the six editions of Economics by Paul Samuelson (McGraw-Hill, New York, 1964).

Purpose of the Chapter

Chapter 1 is designed to introduce the reader to the nature of economics and economic thinking. It presents fundamental definitions and concepts that become the foundation of much of the material that will follow. It explains both the essence of accurate theoretical reasoning and the sort of errors that are often encountered.

Areas for Special Attention

1. The scarcity problem and the need to economize.
2. The problem of making choices between differing wants and goals.
3. The essential nature of theory.
4. The nature of economic reasoning. Inductive and deductive reasoning are often difficult concepts to present. The fallacies should also be illustrated carefully.

Topics for Class Discussion

1. Why is scarcity such a problem when we hear so much about "surpluses" in such fields as agriculture?

2. Isn't it possible to satisfy people at <u>some</u> economic level? What might this level be?
3. Here are two hypothetical speakers; appraise their ideas:
   (a) "My friends, I come here tonight, not to confuse you with mere theories, but to present you with the facts."
   (b) "My friends, I come here tonight, not to confuse you with mere facts, but to present you with a theory."
4. Assume that the price of a certain farm product is very high this year. You are a farmer; will you shift your output next year into this crop? (Note: If all farmers do this, the price may drop.)

True-False Questions

F   1. Economics is the study of what we should make with our unlimited resources.

T   2. Professor John K. Galbraith argues that we should expand public services.

T   3. Choices in economics can involve decisions about how to make the desired goods and services.

F   4. Theories are used only temporarily, before all the facts are known.

T   5. A good theory simplifies the pattern of the relationship between facts.

T   6. Inductive reasoning goes from specific facts toward general principles.

F   7. Deductive reasoning requires more field work to gather facts than inductive reasoning does.

F   8. The purchase of land illustrates the concept of investment in economics.

T   9. The Federal government's debt differs from a family's debt in basic aspects so that comparing the two is fallacious.

F 10. The fallacy <u>post hoc ergo propter hoc</u> means that what is true of the parts may not be true of the whole.

Suggested Answers for Questions at the End of the Chapter

1. The basic economic problem is the problem of using scarce resources to satisfy infinite (or unlimited) human wants.
2. People who save may really be choosing between present and future satisfaction. Presumably they would rather wait until later and end up with more (earning interest on their savings). They may also be saving to buy a large or expensive item (home, luxury car, trip around the world, etc.). In any event, their wants are not satisfied.

3. If a nation's resources are being fully employed, an increase in space exploration means cutting down elsewhere   Other government programs could be cut and men and material could be released for the space program; or, taxes could be raised and the money could be used to buy resources away from private uses into the space program.
4. Cutting taxes to reduce unemployment, what to do about low farm prices, how vigorously the anti-price-fixing laws should be enforced, the question of cutting tariffs, aid to depressed areas, etc.
5. Some form of laboratory or field experiment under controlled conditions is usually possible in the physical sciences. In economics this is often impractical. Therefore theoretical models based on deductive reasoning are often employed. As actual findings from the world become known, the new information can be used to modify the theory.
6. "Other things equal" is to economics what controlled laboratory conditions are to the physical sciences. This allows the analyst to trace the result of a variable (like a tax cut) through a theory without encountering all the miscellaneous disturbances that would arise in the real world.
7. Examples of this fallacy are found in the text. Political orators often make faulty assignments of cause and effect based on their party's (and their opponents') time of taking and leaving office. Examples of this bipartisan activity and students' experiences should be easy to elicit.
8. This is the "facts before conclusions" approach. It opposes the faulty method of starting with a preconceived policy and then seeking an "analysis" that seems to rationalize the policy.
9. Perhaps bad arguments are seen oftener in economics. The issues are close to people's pocketbooks and hearts, the analytical factors involved are often complex, and many groups are seeking popular support for views that may need fallacious reasoning to make them appear palatable.

CHAPTER 2

THE FACTORS OF PRODUCTION

Purpose of the Chapter

Using the traditional "factors of production" terms, this chapter provides some factual understanding of the real resources that underlie economic activity. It makes some references to both progress over time and to comparisons between nations.

3

Areas for Special Attention

1. The descriptive material should not cause difficulty. The part on automation may need some emphasis: It is not merely the use of power, but it is the extensive <u>control</u> of power that differentiates automation from conventional "mass production."
2. The material on Malthus was inserted to include a traditional point that is still regularly quoted. Beyond this, however, the theoretical model cited here illustrates theory itself and also reinforces the material on reasoning in Chapter 1.
3. The law of diminishing returns is elusive to many students. They often find it hard to distinguish <u>extra</u> output from <u>total</u> output.
4. An excellent reference for this chapter is <u>America's Needs and Resources: A New Survey</u> by J. Frederick Dewhurst and Associates (Twentieth Century Fund, New York, 1955).

Topics for Class Discussion

1. Is automation an economic problem (lost jobs, etc.), an economic benefit (higher output), or what? (Note: It may be merely an accelerated version of technological progress, the problems of which can be solved in a high-level full-employment economy.)
2. Was Malthus right? (Note: He applied his model to agricultural, not industrial, economics, and the theory does apply best to the nonindustrial nations today.)
3. Why has the law of diminishing returns not set in on the United States as its population and labor force have gone up? (Note: The law applies to one factor increasing faster than others. Our capital and utilized natural resources have increased along with our labor force.)

True-False Questions

<u>F</u> 1. Brazil's lack of natural resources constitutes a severe block to the nation's economic growth.

<u>F</u> 2. In colonial America about 50 per cent of the labor force worked in agriculture.

<u>T</u> 3. The United States has enough coal to satisfy all its foreseeable needs.

<u>T</u> 4. A sledge hammer and a quarry rock-crushing machine are both capital goods.

<u>F</u> 5. T. R. Malthus used only deductive reasoning.

<u>T</u> 6. The work "entrepreneur" refers to management.

4

F   7. In the past 100 years the output of corn per acre in Illinois has increased almost 30 per cent.

F   8. The law of diminishing returns was discovered in the 1940s when the first automated production systems were introduced.

T   9. Any factor of production can be used as a fixed factor in a problem involving the law of diminishing returns.

T 10. As extra units of a variable factor are added, extra output falls before total output falls.

Suggested Answers for Questions at the End of the Chapter

1. Natural resources
   Capital goods
   Labor
   Management
2. Many nations in South America (notably Brazil) and some in Africa (such as the Congo) would fall in this group. They lack the other factors and the application of technology to the factors.
3. All factor groups have combined to make United States growth what it has been. Especially important has been the fact that current production has almost always been high enough to allow both adequate consumption and accumulation of capital goods for the future.
4. Goods which are used to produce other goods.
5. Management will not knowingly and willingly pay wages that exceed the value of the worker's output or productivity. At the same time an increase in productivity makes possible an increase in wages. In a high-wave market an entrepreneur must make sure productivity is high if the firm is to survive.
6. Students and the instructor will probably have examples in mind. The oil refining and chemical industries probably are among those that most closely approach "automatic factories."
7. With labor-saving devices in the home, women are able to work without causing a stoppage of household work. In addition, the spread of education and the needs of such periods as World War II have dramatized the work-force contributions of women. These factors have all combined to cause society to think affirmatively about the gainful employment of women. Perhaps a severe depression, in which many family men were out of work, would cause a change in this attitude.
8. See point 5 in the chapter summary.
9. It was 190 million in late 1963 and grows at the rate of about 3 million per year. For exact current figures see the Survey of Current Business.

10. Probably almost all firms would fit in here. Good and bad "luck" and economic conditions enter in, but the management of the most successful firms (such as Sears and Ford) have anticipated both problems and opportunities. The reverse is also true.

11. When units of a variable factor are added to a fixed factor, the extra output that results from the extra units of the variable factor may at first rise, but sooner or later the extra output will fall, and eventually total output will fall. This can be illustrated almost limitlessly: The fuel per minute supplied to an engine, the number of workers on a floor-scrubbing job, and perhaps the hours spent studying for an examination.

CHAPTER 3

BUSINESS ORGANIZATIONS

Purpose of the Chapter

The business firm is a basic element in the economic system. This chapter discusses the firm from the standpoint of its form of organization, its ownership and financing, and its management structure.

Areas for Special Attention

The differences between the forms of business organization justify emphasis. The concept of unlimited liability is particularly interesting; perhaps the instructor has observed the not uncommon event of a proprietor or partner losing his home when a business fails. If the annual report of a firm is available (U.S. Steel, Standard Oil of New Jersey, Ford, and many others are generous about sending them for classroom use) it can illustrate realistically the contents of the financial statements. A comprehensive reference source for this chapter is Corporate Financial Policy (4th ed.) by Harry G. Guthmann and Herbert E. Dougall (Prentice-Hall, Englewood Cliffs, N.J., 1962).

Topics for Class Discussion

1. If you were going to start a new small business, which form of organization would you select? Why?

2. Does corporate management usually carry out the desires of the stockholders who own the firm?
3. How do the uses of a balance sheet differ from those of an income statement?

True-False Questions

T 1. A majority of American firms are proprietorships.

F 2. A proprietorship permit from the state is required before a proprietorship business can be started.

T 3. A partner can lose his home if his business debts get large enough and are not paid.

F 4. The law requires a written partnership agreement.

F 5. The 500 largest corporations hold about half the assets of all corporations.

T 6. A charter from the state is required before a corporation can be started.

F 7. All corporations have preferred stock; in addition, some have common stock.

T 8. About 1 per cent of the stockholders usually attend the annual stockholder's meeting of the typical large corporation.

F 9. The director of public relations would be an example of line management from the standpoint of the whole firm.

F 10. The largest asset item on the typical balance sheet is "total receipts from sales."

Suggested Answers for Questions at the End of the Chapter

1. Probably the proprietorship's chief attractions are its simplicity of formation and its lack of legal formalities and "paperwork."

2. The partnership has legal simplicity and the absence of many special reports required of corporations. The partnership does, however, have limited life, unlimited liability, and resultant problems in attracting both skilled employees and money capital.

3. It limits the businessman's loss to the amount he put into the business. His other wealth cannot be taken by business creditors. Without this feature in the corporation the general public would probably be very reluctant to buy ownership shares in business.

4. Common stockholders are often called the "residual" owners of the firm. They get neither profits nor a share of the results of a firm's liquidation until all prior claimants are paid in full.

Preferred stock does provide both a dividend claim and a liquidation claim senior to that of common stockholders. The amount of a preferred stock dividend, however, is usually limited to some stated amount.

5. Bondholders are creditors; they have lent the firm money. They have no control in the firm as long as the firm does what it promised to do (pay them interest and principal and keep the firm sound so that it can continue such payments).

6. A situation in which a person or group outside of management solicits proxies (absentee ballots) from stockholders. The outsider typically claims to be able to do a better job then the current management if given control of the board of directors.

7. The staff performs services for those in the main chain of command. Such services include legal work, public relations, and product planning.

8. It would probably degenerate. There would be a communications breakdown with all orders having to be made at one point. Also, top management would find it very difficult to make decisions for all parts of the firm because of the large distance separating them.

9. Assets might include money, a watch, books, a car, etc. Liabilities would be bills payable and debts owed.

10. In Table 3.2 the item called depreciation and depletion is merely a "provision" or allowance. It indicates a wearing out or using up of an asset, but it is not a current expense.

11. A check of the current financial news will reveal this. In the 1950s and 1960s our "bull" market periods are much more frequent than "bear" markets.

CHAPTER 4

LABOR ORGANIZATIONS

Purpose of the Chapter

This chapter continues the institutional background set up in the previous one. Unions are both a major participant in many economic matters and the subject of a substantial body of legislation. An understanding of the basic concepts concerning labor organization thus has value for its own sake. In addition, this material provides some foundation in the nature of the real world. This should be desirable, since it precedes the more theoretical material following. The theories can often lose their connection with human affairs, and, if they do so, full understanding may suffer.

Areas for Special Attention

1. The different functions of the federation, the international, and the local are often difficult for the beginning student to comprehend.
2. The noneconomic aspects of unions are often not understood.
3. The material on public policy can be expanded or summarized by the instructor. Its presentation in the text is designed to give the flavor of detail without attempting to be encyclopedic. Since this area of legislation is relatively active, some consideration seems appropriate.

An excellent source book for this chapter is <u>Labor</u> by Neil Chamberlain (McGraw-Hill, New York, 1958).

Topics for Class Discussion

1. If you went to work in a plant where there was no union shop, would you join the union?
2. Should unions be regulated by government more than they are at present?
3. Why might an employer <u>wish</u> to pay above-average wages? (Note: To get and keep above-average workers. In some industries such skilled labor is more important than in others).

True-False Questions

<u>F</u> 1. Unions first appeared in the United States in the early 1900s.
<u>F</u> 2. Samuel Gompers founded the CIO.
<u>T</u> 3. The CIO emphasized the industrial-union type of organization.
<u>F</u> 4. Labor unions experienced a fast growth during the late 1950s.
<u>T</u> 5. Total strike time per year is usually less than 1 per cent of the total time all workers work per year.
<u>T</u> 6. Chief Justice Shaw in 1842 revised the doctrine of criminal conspiracy.
<u>F</u> 7. Yellow-dog contracts are those which require workers to seek injunctions in court.
<u>T</u> 8. The representation election was established by the Wagner Act.

T   9. The Taft-Hartley Act requires unions to bargain in good faith with management.
F   10. The Landrum-Griffin Act contains the provision allowing states to pass "right-to-work" laws.

Suggested Answers for Questions at the End of the Chapter

1. Gompers sought the practical goals of better wages, hours, and working conditions. He did not emphasize general reform of society and the economy. He is also known as an advocate of craft unions.

2. In simple terms, the AFL adhered to the craft union idea and the CIO advocated industrial unions.

3. They will have to organize the technicians and clerical workers. These are groups which are growing; traditional manual labor is not growing as much.

4. The AFL-CIO is a federation whose members are unions. The federation is a spokesman for member unions, but it does not actually bargain with management.

5. He represents the workers in their grievances with foremen and other management personnel. He may also collect dues and recruit members. The steward is the main daily contact members have with their union.

6. Other standards lack measurability and impartiality. They include merit (ability, performance on the job—hard to gauge on machine-paced jobs), need (compare man with sick wife to man with ten children), cooperative attitude (favoritism), preference for youth, etc.

7. They reduced the effectiveness of strikes, which are tied in with bargaining power.

8. The Wagner Act assumed that unions are weak and needed special rights ensured by law. The Taft-Hartley Act was passed after unions had gained strength and imposes duties on them (such as bargaining in good faith, like employers had to under the Wagner Act); it also regulates the use of their power (secondary boycott prohibition).

9. (a) Union members have the right to attend meetings, speak and vote.
   (b) Unions must have a constitution and must keep careful financial records.
   (c) Internationals must allow members to vote for officers at least once every five years.
   (d) Unions cannot lend over $2,000 to their officers.
   (e) Stealing union funds is a new Federal crime.

(f) It is a crime for union officers to take bribes from employers.

(g) See text on Taft-Hartley amendments.

10. This has been tried in some nations (such as Australia). Its chief disadvantage is the fact that free collective bargaining with a final decision by the parties themselves is often lost. The parties work to influence the arbitrators and the public rather than reach an agreement themselves. It might, of course, result in a positive decision where one was not forthcoming. Dissatisfied workers could still walk out in wildcat strikes, however. The apparent advantages of such arbitration—especially on a compulsory basis—might well prove illusory. A major nationwide strike often occasions suggestions for a Federal law requiring arbitration.

PART II. THE DETERMINATION
OF NATIONAL INCOME

CHAPTER 5

THE NATIONAL INCOME

Purpose of the Chapter

This chapter presents the mechanics of national income measurement. It seeks to explain the concepts behind the published totals. Price changes affect year-to-year income comparisons; therefore, a discussion of price indexes and their use is included.

Areas for Special Attention

An understanding of the GNP is basic. It should be stressed more than the contents of the other measures. The measure called "net national product" (GNP minus capital consumption) is omitted in the text. This omission reflects the Department of Commerce's growing practice and the author's desire not to add nonessential detail. The process of lowering the current dollar figure of later high-priced GNPs to constant dollars of an earlier year is called "deflating" the BNP. Current figures can be found in the July issue (each year) of the Survey of Current Business. Another reference source is National Income by Sam Rosen (Holt, Rinehart and Winston, New York, 1963).

Topics for Class Discussion

1. Does a rising GNP (at constant prices) prove a nation is better off economically? (Note: Consider population increases and also the things like superhighway interchanges that may be required merely because of our increasing crowding into urban areas).
2. Depreciation of capital goods is deducted from GNP before we get NI. Can you think of other wearing out that is not deducted? (Note: We cut down trees, burn up coal, and perhaps wear out people—think of a teacher's eyes. This can illustrate the fact that all the measurements are somewhat arbitrary).

3. In 1939 the GNP was about $100 B, and 1939 prices equal 100. The 1963 GNP was about $600 B, and prices, relative to 1939, equal about 200. How much was the 1963 GNP in 1939 dollars? (Note: $600 B/2.0 = $300 B.)

True-False Questions

T   1. The national income arises from production.
F   2. The value of housewives' work at home is counted in the TNP.
T   3. Consumption is the largest component of the GNP.
F   4. Social security payments are counted as part of government spending for goods and services.
F   5. The corporation income tax is an indirect business tax.
T   6. Personal income taxes are subtracted from PI to get DPI.
F   7. Prices in 1961 went up more rapidly in the United States than they did in Brazil.
T   8. Prices declined during the 1880s.
T   9. Debtors benefit from inflation more than creditors.
F 10. Rapid inflation can ensure economic growth in developing nations.

Suggested Answers for Questions at the End of the Chapter

1. It enters into the value of the final product shipped. This can be either C, I, or G, depending on who buys it.
2. Most is consumption (such as personal pleasure trips). The cost of a businessman's trip would enter into the value of the final products of his firm. The cost of transporting military personnel on duty would be government spending for goods and services.
3. (a) Deduct capital consumption allowances and indirect business taxes from GNP.
   (b) Add up all factor incomes before income taxes (wages, salaries, profits, etc.).
4. They affect the significance of comparisons between different years. Adjusting the GNP for price changes solves this problem.
5. Personal taxes are deducted from PI to get DPI. People can actually spend or save their DPI.
6. Debtors are helped and businessmen and farmers often find their prices rising faster than their costs. Creditors, retired persons on fixed pensions, and others whose economic welfare is tied to fixed dollar incomes are hurt.

7. Some inflation is compatible with economic progress, and some argue that inflation does encourage current spending for C and I. It is hard to prove historically, however, that inflation is an essential precondition of economic progress. Other incentives (product improvements, favorable taxes) can give the needed stimulus.
8. Services.
9. It is hard to draw an exact quantitative line. Mild or creeping inflation might be 1 or 2 per cent per year; it might even be as high as 5. Rapid inflation would be a doubling each year; it would probably even include a steady rise of much over 10 per cent in the United States. In practice, there might be a drying up of long-term loan funds (needed for some investment, such as new home purchases) if the price rise exceeded the interest rate.

CHAPTER 6

TOTAL SPENDING AND NATIONAL INCOME

Purpose of the Chapter

The forces determining national income are presented in this chapter. The concepts here are vital in providing for an understanding of public policy issues relating to unemployment, tax cuts, government spending, and other macroeconomic points.

Areas for Special Attention

The subject matter of this chapter is perhaps more rigorous than that of any chapter in the book. At this point, however, understanding can begin to go below the surface of the earlier descriptive and institutional material.

A basic feature of this book's presentation is the omission of the graphs often employed. This was done because of the author's feeling that elementary students very often miss an understanding of analysis as they strive for a mastery of mechanics. If the instructor wishes to use graphs, he will probably find them more comprehensible as presented step by step in class then they would be as read by most students in the text.

Probably the multiplier is the key to this chapter. Certainly its importance can hardly be overstated. Find the current GNP and forecast the increase new spending would cause with various values for the MPC and MPS.

A good reference source for this chapter is A Guide to Keynes by Alvin Hansen (McGraw-Hill, New York, 1953).

Topics for Class Discussion

1. There is evidence to indicate that people's consumption exceeded their disposable income in 1933. Can you explain this? (Note: Incomes were very low and people used up savings. This should have given a strong multiplier, except for very low levels of investment and government spending.)
2. Would a wage cut be a good way to lower unemployment? (Note: It might encourage some employers and could lead to price cuts that could raise sales. These expensive effects, however, would probably be counteracted by fear on the part of most workers of further wage and price cuts. This negative expectation would cause them to cease as much buying as they could; especially, they would quit buying durable goods on credit. This could easily make unemployment even worse.)
3. What would happen if spending was cut by 1 billion dollars? (Note: GNP would go down more than 1 billion dollars; the multiplier works in reverse.)

True-False Questions

F   1. Keynes was more concerned with the long run than with the short run.

F   2. Savings automatically flow into the investment stream.

T   3. The marginal propensity to consume is usually less than the average propensity to consume.

T   4. The marginal propensity to save is usually smaller than the marginal propensity to consume.

F   5. Consumption as measured by the APC was unusually high during the full-employment period of World War II.

T   6. "Easy" credit encourages consumption spending.

T   7. Surveys of consumer buying intentions are conducted by the Federal Reserve.

F   8. A higher corporation income tax would raise investment.

F   9. Autonomous investment causes the accelerator to work.

T   10. If the MPC is $0.66\frac{2}{3}$, the multiplier is 3.

Suggested Answers for Questions at the End of the Chapter

1. In a complicated economy based on money flows and containing saving, desire to work and consume may not always match up with willingness to spend. If people fear bad economic conditions in the future, it makes sense for them as individuals to save now so that their later satisfactions will be possible. If all do this though, spending will decline and the feared decline will become a reality. Once in a depression, even those with money may fear to spend it and thereby exhaust their purchasing power.
2. The level of spending during the period.
3. APC considers <u>total</u> income, while MPC considers <u>changes</u> in income. When income changes, there is an old APC, an MPC, and a new APC.
4. Availability of good, availability of credit, size of built-up personal savings, desire for goods, and consumer confidence.
5. The profit outlook is most important. Low interest rates and low corporation taxes are favorable factors for high investment.
6. Some level of GNP can be said to represent the volume of spending required to provide full employment. The actual GNP is usually not at this level; it is almost a happy accident if the actual GNP and the full-employment GNP are the same.
7. This is the case in which an increase in consumption causes a <u>greater</u> relative increase in investment. This happens because there is a need to expand the total volume of capital goods in addition to the more usual need to replace the capital goods that wear out.
8. The multiplier is 4 $(1/qr = 4)$. Thus with the information presented here we could expect the GNP to rise to \$640 billion.
9. If one person tries to save more, he can do it. If all try to save more, they will cut down consumption, income, <u>and savings</u>.

CHAPTER 7

THE MONETARY SYSTEM AND NATIONAL INCOME

Purpose of the Chapter

Money is basic to an economy. This chapter explains the uses of money, presents the basis of our money and banking system, and shows how the Federal Reserve can change the money supply.

Areas for Special Attention

Perhaps the main point for emphasis in this chapter is the fact that our money supply is consciously managed. Many people accept the money supply as something that must have been handed down from the past, and it is merely carried on "as is" now. If we can show here how the money supply is constantly adjusted to meet the needs of the economy, we will dispel any such misconceptions.

The "backing" of money is also not well understood by most citizens. The place of gold needs to be put into perspective. An excellent book can usually be ordered free in classroom quantities from the Board of Governors of the Federal Reserve System. It is entitled The Federal Reserve System—Purposes and Functions (1963 edition).

Topics for Class Discussion

1. What keeps people from making a "run" on banks—that is, rushing to draw out cash all at once causing banks to fail? (Note: This happened often in the 1930s. It is less likely to happen now because of the FDIC and general confidence in our economy.)
2. Should our money have more "backing" with gold and silver or other items of value?
3. Can the banks and the Federal Reserve actually produce money?

True-False Questions

T   1. Money is used even by primitive societies.
T   2. As prices go up, the value of money goes down.
F   3. Silver certificates constitute the largest segment of our money supply.
F   4. Savings accounts are part of our money supply.
F   5. All banks are required to be members of the Federal Reserve System.
F   6. The account called "deposits" is typically the largest asset of a bank.
T   7. Lower reserve requirements encourage banks to make loans.
T   8. The twelve Federal Reserve banks deal mainly with commercial banks rather than with the public.
T   9. Turnover of bank deposits is highest in New York City.
F   10. Stock market margin requirements are usually raised when stock prices go down.

Suggested Answers for Questions at the End of the Chapter

1. Medium of exchange, standard of value, and store of value.
2. Barter would be used in the beginning. Later, commodities would probably come into use as a medium of exchange. These would be items of value in themselves which possess such traits as storability (metal), portability (precious stones), and divisibility (tobacco).
3. Bills, coins, and checking accounts.
4. To receive deposits and make loans. By making loans a bank can create money within limits imposed by reserve requirements.
5. To insure repayment of deposits up to $10,000 in the event of bank failure. This has helped produce a high level of depositor confidence in our insured banks.
6. The amount of cash and Federal Reserve bank balances a bank has in excess of the amount required by law. This amount is stated as a percentage of deposits in the bank.
7. When they make a loan they produce a new deposit for the borrower without reducing anyone else's deposit. (Note: On rare occasions when borrowers take bills or coin this is extra money in circulation outside banks. This also "creates" new money without reducing that already in circulation.)
8. They issue currency, examine member banks, clear checks between banks, hold United States government deposits, and (most important) they regulate the size of the money supply through open-market operations, reserve-requirement changes, and interest-rate changes.
9. The Fed buys and sells United States bonds (secondhand ones) on the open market for such bonds. They buy bonds to put more money into the economy; they sell bonds to reduce the amount of money. These two choices are often called "ease" and "restraint" of the money supply.
10. "Margins" are the "down payment" on stocks. If they are lowered (lowest usually used is 50 per cent), stock buying is encouraged. If they are raised (highest possible is 100 per cent), stock buying is discouraged.
11. The dollar is expressed as fixed in relation to gold, since the official (since 1934) price of gold is $35 per ounce. If we ran short of gold, we might have to raise the price to attract more gold. This raising of gold's price is a lowering of the dollar's value. Currently we need to have gold stocks equal to 25 per cent of the value of Federal Reserve notes and 25 per cent of the amount of member banks' accounts at the Federal Reserve

banks. We have been losing gold to other nations since 1957. (Reasons: Military spending abroad, foreign aid spending, and investment spending in other countries.)

CHAPTER 8

PROSPERITY AND DEPRESSION

Purpose of the Chapter

Economic fluctuations have held the attention of economists for well over a century. This chapter considers the nature of the business cycle, especially as it has occurred in recent years. It also presents the public policy measures that now exist to control the excesses of cyclical fluctuations.

Areas for Special Attention

1. The fact that some items (durables, etc.) fluctuate most should be emphasized.
2. The causes of or reasons for the cycle should be presented as a series of factors working together. At times some may be more dominant than others.
3. Fiscal policy and the debt are often misunderstood. A strong statement in favor of an active fiscal policy is to be found in The Economics of Employment by Abba P. Lerner (McGraw-Hill, New York, 1951).

Topics for Class Discussion

1. Should monetary policy be directly under the control of the President of the United States? (Now it is controlled by the largely independent Board of Governors of the Federal Reserve.) (Note: The argument here is between a system directly responsive to the current administration and one with a built-in check and balance on the President.)
2. Have we solved the problem of depressions?
3. Is the national debt a problem? Should we be striving to reduce it—or increase it?

True-False Questions

<u>T</u> 1. The greatest depression in American history started in late 1929.

<u>F</u> 2. Between 1947 and 1963 the United States had only two recessions.

<u>T</u> 3. During recent recessions the unemployment rate has exceeded 6 per cent.

<u>T</u> 4. During a recession businessmen usually wish to reduce inventories.

<u>T</u> 5. A stock market decline is actually capable of triggering a recession.

<u>F</u> 6. Congress has closer control over monetary policy than it does over fiscal policy.

<u>F</u> 7. To control inflation the Fed buys bonds.

<u>F</u> 8. If interest rates go up, prices of secondhand bonds go up.

<u>T</u> 9. A 1 billion dollar tax cut will probably have a less expensive effect than a 1 billion dollar government spending increase.

<u>F</u> 10. During a recession the government should run a surplus in order to reduce the national debt and thus restore public confidence.

Suggested Answers for Questions at the End of the Chapter

1. The recent recessions have been far less severe and they have been shorter. Unemployment reached 25 per cent in the early thirties, but it usually has not gone much over 6 per cent in the postwar recessions.

2. By fluctuations in various published economic series. Among the best are personal income and industrial production.

3. Purchase of durables can be postponed by consumers when their income or expectations are down. Conversely during prosperous periods people catch up on such items.

4. They tend to rise during the upswing, thus accentuating it. They are liquidated during the downswing, further lowering production.

5. Expectations can be self-fulfilling. If people as a whole expect good times and thus are willing to spend more (especially incurring debts) and save less, the "good times" are more likely to come. The reverse is also true.

6. It is an act which states that it is the responsibility of the Federal government to adopt policies that will promote maximum employment. It also sets up the three-man Council of Economic Advisors for the President and it provides for regular Economic Reports of the President to the Congress.

7. They are related inversely. Higher interest rates lower the market values of older bonds that return fixed dollar interest payments based on lower percentage rates.
8. This is the Federal Reserve policy (used extensively in the 1950s) of confining open-market operations to the very shortest term (usually ninety-one days) Treasury debt instruments. This was done to minimize the effects on long-term interest rates which some officials thought should be set by the free market. Critics of the policy argue that it restricts the scope of open-market operations; they also contend that Federal Reserve policy should influence interest rates.
9. The spending would give the stronger multiplier. All of the 1 billion dollars would go into the spending stream. With a tax cut, part would be saved immediately. If the MPC was 0.75, only three-quarters of the billion dollars would go initially into the spending stream. (Note: The multiplier of 4 would thus work on 0.75 billion dollars, giving a final income increase of 3 billion dollars from the tax cut—an effective multiplier of 3 based on the tax cut itself.)
10. This would not be a neutral policy. In recessions, tax losses (caused by lower incomes) would call for higher tax rates to keep the budget balanced. These higher taxes would make the recession more severe. Conversely an inflationary boom would call for a tax cut if a strict balance of the budget, rather than a surplus, is wanted.

CHAPTER 9

ECONOMIC GROWTH

Purpose of the Chapter

This chapter seeks to identify the nature of economic growth and to explain something of the sources of growth. Further, it suggests ways to encourage growth.

Areas for Special Attention

1. The difference between the cycle and growth should be emphasized.
2. Growth rests on the physical factors. It also requires a spending level adequate to utilize these factors.

21

3. The growth rate can be influenced by both private and public decisions and policies.

A reference source for this chapter is <u>The Theory of Economic Growth</u> by William A. Lewis (Richard D. Irwin, Homewood, Ill., 1955).

Topics for Class Discussion

1. Is economic growth as important a goal for public policy as full employment?
2. What is the "cost" of economic growth? (Note: Harder work, less consumption and more investment, etc.)
3. How could the economic growth rate of the United States be increased?

True-False Questions

T   1. A true measure of growth should consider prices.
F   2. Economic growth can be accurately measured from one year to the next.
F   3. In 1947 about 10 per cent of all Americans over fourteen years of age were illiterate.
T   4. In the 1947-1951 period, business fixed investment was about 10 per cent of the GNP.
T   5. Our economic growth rate has averaged 3 per cent.
F   6. The failure of research spending to increase in amount has slowed our economic growth.
T   7. Prosperity encourages economic growth. (Note: It is possible to conceive of prosperity and full employment in a low-growth, low-investment, subsistence economy.)
F   8. Under the 1962 law, firms can reduce their taxes by 7 per cent of their before-tax income.
T   9. Investment under the 7 per cent tax credit is subject to the multiplier effect.
T 10. In 1962 depreciation "guidelines" were shortened.

Suggested Answers for Questions at the End of the Chapter

1. The actual magnitude of GNP changes in physical terms is obscured if price changes are ignored.
2. The cycle is short (recently about four years), while growth is a long-term phenomenon.

3. Education stimulates growth by raising people's skills and thus raising their output. Growth, by raising incomes, could be expected to make it easier for people to educate their children.
4. The untapped resources and the modest starting point are in the primitive nation's favor. Despite this, however, the well-developed nation has a big advantage: It can afford to save part of current output for investment that will raise future output.
5. They have done well, but they did start (after World War II) from a much lower base.
6. Recession periods have below-average investment spending. Since present capacity is unused, there is less incentive to build new capacity.
7. It is increasing rapidly, both in amount and as a percentage of GNP. This should spur economic growth.
8. It will raise growth by encouraging investment spending.
9. Shorter depreciation periods (higher annual depreciation allowances) encourage economic growth. This is because they allow a firm to keep more of its year's money receipts. At the same time, they encourage the spending of this money in order to permit taking advantage of the larger allowances in the future.

PART III. ECONOMICS AND THE WORLD

CHAPTER 10

ECONOMIC RELATIONSHIPS BETWEEN NATIONS

Purpose of the Chapter

This chapter seeks to present the logic underlying interregional and international trade. It also discusses barriers to trade in the form of tariffs and quotas. Further, it considers the recent American balance of trade and balance of payments situation.

Areas for Special Attention

1. The logic of comparative advantage is not easy to grasp. If students can give an accurate answer to discussion topic 1 below, they should be on the right track.
2. On the issue of low foreign wages undermining American workers, encourage students to realize their fallacy by formulating protariff arguments which a protectionist in a low-wage nation might use.
3. The difference between balance of trade and balance of payments should be stressed. Reference: <u>An International Economy</u> by Gunnar Myrdal (Harper & Row, New York, 1956).

Topics for Class Discussion

1. If the United States were more productive (more units of output with less units of factor of production input) than all other nations, would international trade still be advantageous to us? [Note: Yes. We should let others produce products where our superiority was (for example) two-to-one so that we could concentrate on items where we had a four-to-one advantage.] Political and good-will advantages might also enter the discussion.
2. The United States has the world's highest wages, yet many other nations have tariffs higher than ours (compare the 25 per cent Common Market tariff on United States cars with the 6 per cent United States tariff on European cars). What arguments might a politician in a low-wage nation use to promote such tariffs?

3. Should the United States attempt to enter the Common Market? (Note: The Trade Expansion Act of 1962 allows us to negotiate mutual tariff reductions. If these succeed, they could pave the way for more cooperation.)

True-False Questions

F 1. Nations should produce only products in which they have an absolute advantage over other nations.
T 2. Worker output is a major determinant of wages.
F 3. Gold outflows from the United States are caused by our unfavorable balance of trade.
T 4. Most economists favor free trade.
F 5. In the 1830-1860 period the South favored high tariffs.
F 6. France has refused to join the Common Market.
T 7. A nation can raise exports by cutting tariffs.
T 8. The quota has been used to limit imports of fish.
T 9. Canadian exports prospered after the value of the Canadian dollar was lowered.
F 10. The International Monetary Fund was set up under the Common Market.

Suggested Answers for Questions at the End of the Chapter

1. It is helped. Internal free trade lets regions specialize in the products they make best. By doing so, and trading, all parts have more.
2. Absolute advantage is the case in which one area (or nation) can produce a good with less units of the factors of production than another area. Florida has this advantage over Vermont in the raising of oranges because of its weather.
3. Comparative advantage involves the relative degree of absolute advantage a nation (or an area) has when more than one product is considered. Florida apparently has absolute advantage over Vermont in both oranges and cattle; probably its comparative advantage is greater in the case of oranges. An area should specialize in the products for which its comparative advantage is greatest or for which its comparative disadvantage is least.
4. No. Presumably the low wages are based on generally lower productivity. We import products for which their comparative disadvantage is least. It is logical for the United States to import goods of low price made with hand labor (such as some baskets, for example) so that our workers can concentrate on products (such as bulldozers) which can support high wages.

5. The trade balance refers to imports and exports only. The payments balance includes capital flows, gifts, and gold flows also. (See Table 10.1 for details.)

6. This traditional term is still used since selling more than you buy sounds "favorable." Eventually, of course, your balance could get so favorable that other nations ran out of gold; at this point a less favorable or unfavorable balance would be in the nation's long-run interest.

7. A few new industries or defense industries might need tariffs (they could also be helped more openly by direct payments from the government, if they are so essential. The disadvantages of lessening the benefits of trade and of creating international ill will stand against these advantages.

8. It is the six-nation European group that is lowering internal trade barriers and working toward economic (and perhaps political and social) unity.

9. They are usually used when a tariff would have to be very high (perhaps 100 per cent of the import's value) in order to keep the import out. Such a high tariff can spark domestic consumer opposition, where a quota can do the job more quietly.

10. Currency devaluation stimulates a nation's exports, since its money becomes cheaper for other nations to buy. Devaluation is limited by the fact that other countries can block this effect by devaluing their own money.

CHAPTER 11

THE CHOICE OF AN ECONOMIC SYSTEM
IN UNDERDEVELOPED NATIONS

Purpose of the Chapter

This chapter combines discussion of comparative economic systems with considering the problems of the developing low-income nations. It presents the features of the other systems, notably communism, and something of the arguments made on behalf of them to new countries.

Areas for Special Attention

1. The developing nations often lack resources, and this presents a real dilemma. If they were all laden with untapped riches, perhaps

their problems would be easier to solve. The fact that population can increase and soak up all economic advance is another point to stress.

2. Perhaps the chief feature of a communistic economy is the fact that the market is not given the chance to choose between consumer goods and capital goods—between present and future. This may raise investment, but it eliminates free decisions and leads to "black markets" and shortages.

A classic sourcebook in this field is Capitalism, Socialism and Democracy by Joseph A. Schumpeter (Harper & Row, New York, 1950).

Topics for Class Discussion

1. Suggest the broad elements of a development program that might help guide a developing nation.
2. Should our government spend tax money on helping underdeveloped nations? (Note: If it makes them into customers, it might repay us.)
3. How do communistic and capitalistic economies really differ?

True-False Questions

T   1. Some nations have an annual income of under $100 per person.

F   2. It is desirable for a small nation to specialize in a single crop.

F   3. Recent attempts have shown that most illiterate people in underdeveloped nations are untrainable.

T   4. A tax based on ability to pay can help stimulate a poor economy.

F   5. If a nation can establish a steel industry, its progress is assured. (Note: Some have thought so and now have conspicuously unsuccessful steel industries—and still low growth.)

F   6. By raising birth rates, and thus increasing the labor force, economic growth can always be aided.

T   7. Russia has a "foreign aid" program.

T   8. Russian communism has diverted resources away from the consumer sector into the investment government sector.

F   9. Low prices are used in Russia to keep consumption down.

T   10. The Russian carrot crop represents that nation's recent discovery of free markets.

Suggested Answers for Questions at the End of the Chapter

1. Income under approximately $300 to $500 per person per year, high death rate, low rate of economic growth, heavy dependence on agriculture, poor housing, inadequate food, insufficient clothing, etc.
2. The "rising expectations" brought about by recent advances in communication and brought into focus by political independence in some areas.
3. Transportation, communication, and education. The last is probably most important, and it may rest on some health improvements.
4. Unstable government, certain religious practices, poor health.
5. A tax system weighing mainly on the poor (with a high MPC) can make the whole economy sluggish and hold back development.
6. Perhaps some are overpopulated relative to resources. Hopefully, however, some improvement is possible everywhere.
7. Excess population growth can consume all extra GNP and leave the per capita income as low as ever.
8. Some political gains may come from showy projects that do not aid in basic development. An international airport raises the prestige of a nation (and admittedly gives better transportation— at least for those who fly), but basic education might build more long-term gains. Both types of aid have their place.
9. Central decisions characterize communism. In free markets, on the other hand, the price system reflects consumer and investor preferences.
10. Democratic socialism is voted in and out. It is compatible with a high level of personal freedom. Communism is in the totalitarian authoritarian tradition; it allows for no opposition. Both systems have government ownership; democratic socialism allows for free choice and is responsive to free markets.

PART IV. PRINCIPLES OF PRICE

CHAPTER 12

THE WHOLE ECONOMY AND
THE INDIVIDUAL PRODUCTIVE UNIT

Purpose of the Chapter

This chapter attempts to introduce the concept of general equilibrium—the mutual relationships between prices and outputs of all products. It also presents the idea that prices direct the uses of resources throughout the economy.

Areas for Special Attention

The principal concept to emphasize is the fact that any purchase can have widespread effects on the economy. The major dislocations of wars show up this fact clearly, but it always exists. Price changes reflect the varying choice patterns of consumers.

Topics for Class Discussion

1. What effects would an increase in the United States space program have on the economy?
2. Do flexible rather than rigid prices aid an economy in adjusting to changing consumption patterns?
3. What business has no effect on interstate commerce?

True-False Questions

F 1. Macroeconomics emphasizes individual economic units.

F 2. Total consumption spending is a microeconomic variable.

T 3. Leon Walras was a pioneer in the study of general equilibrium.

T 4. The final general equilibrium is the result of conflicting forces.

T 5. High consumer acceptance of the product of one industry tends to raise the level of national income.

F 6. The study of inputs and outputs has been applied mainly to peacetime periods.

F 7. The Civil War cotton shortage lowered the sales of the Irish linen industry.

29

T   8. The Civil War cotton shortage raised the sales of the English farm-tool industry.

F   9. When the production in one industry drops, the production of substitute products tends to drop.

T   10. When the production in one industry rises, the production in industries making its inputs tends to rise.

Suggested Answers for Questions at the End of the Chapter

1. Macroeconomics is the branch of economics that concentrates on the overall level of economic activity, such as the size of national income. Economic wholes or aggregates, such as total consumption, are emphasized.

2. Microeconomics is the branch of the subject that concentrates on the price, output, and wage decisions of individual firms and workers. The individual units within the economy are emphasized.

3. On the macroeconomic level, small units act together to determine totals. On the microeconomic level the activities of small units affect other units (and perhaps finally the whole economy) directly and indirectly. For example, if a firm goes out of business, its input firms may be hurt, while substitute producers are helped.

4. This is done for the sake of simplicity. In addition, the secondary effects may be so small and hard to trace that they can be ignored. Further, the business decision maker must often decide on the basis of his own firm's interest; he may not be able to allow broader aspects of the decision to influence him. The dropping of a product line to permit a firm's survival illustrates this point.

5. Inputs are the things a firm or industry must buy from others to support its production. Outputs are the products a firm or industry turns out. One industry's output may be another industry's input. Input-output relationships may be mutual. For example the can industry needs some paint as inputs, while the paint industry needs cans as part of its inputs.

6. Wars illustrate economic interdependence. While they often stimulate total production, they lead to shortages as supplies are cut off or diverted away from civilian industries. They may thus lower some types of production, but they stimulate the search for substitutes.

7. Most relationships will fall into these categories: customers, suppliers, and competitors. The manufacture of motortrucks is an industry for which illustrations of each of these three will readily come to mind.

CHAPTER 13

THE LAW OF SUPPLY AND DEMAND

Purpose of the Chapter

In this chapter the basis of price theory is presented. Supply and demand relationships form the heart of microeconomics, and an understanding of them is essential to the remaining chapters.

Areas for Special Attention

1. The difference between a change in demand and a change in quantity demanded is basic. Better styling of new automobiles raises demand; lower prices raises quantity demanded.
2. Elasticity of demand is also very important.

A good reference for this chapter and also Chapters 14, 15, 17, and 18 is <u>Intermediate Economic Analysis</u> by John Due (Richard D. Irwin, Homewood, Ill., 1961).

Topics for Class Discussion

1. What products have relatively elastic demand for you?
2. Suppose color television sets are simultaneously improved in quality and cut in price. How would this be shown with demand curves?
3. Why is competition so important in letting the law of supply and demand work? (Note: A monopolist can set a price to maximize profits; this is not necessarily the supply and demand price. The soft-drink illustration in the text introduces this concept.)

True-False Questions

<u>F</u>   1. Supply and demand determine all prices. (Note: In competitive markets, etc.)

<u>T</u>   2. Demand is defined as the amount of a good buyers will actually buy at any one time at each of the possible prices that might be charged.

<u>F</u>   3. An increase in buyers' incomes would be represented by sliding up the demand curve.

<u>F</u>   4. The law of diminishing returns states that more will be bought at a lower price than a higher one.

<u>F</u>   5. Hotter weather, other things equal, raises the "quantity demanded" for soft drinks.

T   6. An increase in demand is shown by a shift to the right in the demand curve.

T   7. An increase in supply is shown by a shift to the right in the supply curve.

T   8. The availability of substitutes makes demand more elastic.

T   9. An increase in demand raises price and quantity sold.

F 10. A decrease in supply lowers price and quantity sold.

Suggested Answers for Questions at the End of the Chapter

1. Other things equal, prospective buyers will usually offer to buy more of a commodity at any one time as the price goes down; other things equal prospective sellers will usually offer to sell more of a commodity at any one time as the price goes up. In competitive markets price and output will tend to be determined by the point at which the buyers' and sellers' offers are alike.

2. Perhaps some expensive perfume, jewelry, furs, and even cars would fit in here.

3. No. The monopolist could set the price where it maximized profits, based on demand. (Costs would also enter in.)

4. Demand is the amount of a good buyers will actually buy at any one time at each of the possible prices that might be charged. It is based on consumer's desire plus ability and willingness to pay.

5. Elastic. A 50 per cent reduction in price causes a tenfold quantity increase. Also, more ($25) is spent at the lower price than is spent at the higher price ($5).

6. Urgent need and no substitute makes demand inelastic. The non-urgency of need and the presence of good substitutes makes demand elastic.

7. A great need to sell makes supply inelastic. Such need is based on need for money, expense of storage, and perishability of the product. Elastic supply thus might be associated with a seller with adequate funds and a storable product.

8. These things might happen:
   (a) A "black market" could develop in which sales were made illegally at the $2 price.
   (b) There could be shortages of the product as people anxiously awaited the few units sellers would offer for $1 and then bought them suddenly when they appeared.
   (c) Rationing on the basis of need could be instituted by the government. In this way the short supply could be allocated. Informal rationing could also be practiced by merchants, with favored customers getting the scarce items.

9. High prices encourage production and also "ration" the valuable product (only those who really want it—and can pay—get it). Low prices encourage consumption and discourage further production of a surplus product.
10. See graphs in the text.

PART V. THE COMPETITIVE FIRM

CHAPTER 14

COSTS FOR THE BUSINESS FIRM

Purpose of the Chapter

The concept that one thing must usually be given up to have another is basic in economics. The sacrifices involved are measured by the cost of productive resources. This chapter considers costs and especially emphasizes the relationship between costs and the rate of output.

Areas for Special Attention

1. The costs that do not involve current spending, such as depreciation and opportunity costs, are often hard to understand for the beginning reader.
2. Each size of firm has its low cost point. One size firm has the lowest point of all.

Topics for Class Discussion

1. What is the opportunity cost of going to an institution of higher education?
2. A firm has a net worth of $100,000. Its profit was $4,000 last year. If the rate of interest is 4 per cent, how would opportunity cost affect profit? (Note: It would eliminate it. The firm shows book profit, but no economic profit.)
3. Are there any economic forces that push firms toward the most efficient plant size?

True-False Questions

<u>T</u> 1. Labor is an expenditure cost.
<u>F</u> 2. Depreciation is an expenditure cost.
<u>T</u> 3. Smoke from plants that soils laundry is a social cost.
<u>F</u> 4. Fixed costs increase as output increases.
<u>F</u> 5. Railroads have relatively low fixed costs.
<u>T</u> 6. Depreciation can be either a fixed or a variable cost.

F 7. Marginal cost cuts through the lowest point of average fixed costs.

T 8. Average cost is always above average variable cost.

F 9. Low management pay usually causes the AC of a small firm to be lower than the AC of a larger firm.

T 10. Linear programming can be used to find the lowest-cost method of production.

Suggested Answers for Questions at the End of the Chapter

1. It is the value of that which must be given up in order to have (or produce) an item.

2. They could be charged to the firm or industries involved. Thus they could be passed on to consumers of the products that cause the trouble. These costs are hard to measure, however, and also such charges would also stir up much business resentment. Other alternatives might also come to mind (such as government payments to persons harmed).

3. Barber Shop: His wages in other employment.
   Auto manufacturer: Interest that could be earned on the money invested in the firm.

4. Labor and materials are major variable costs. Rent and property taxes illustrate fixed costs.

5. Most decisions concern ''more'' or ''less''; they are seldom concerned with ''all'' or ''none.'' A going concern changes its rate of output often and marginal cost is important in guiding such decisions.

6. MC is an extra item added to a series; AC is the average of the whole series. A falling average (AC) cannot begin to rise until an extra item (MC) above average has been added into the series.

7. Yes. If the price is above AVC, at least the firm can pay part of its fixed costs. Refusing the business means paying none of fixed costs. Strategic considerations might affect this issue (will you ever be able to get a higher price in the future after selling cheaply now?).

8. They can get skilled management and specialized equipment. These high-fixed-cost items can give a very low AC when spread over many units.

9. It allows management to select the lowest-cost alternative when the date is extensive and complicated.

CHAPTER 15

PURE COMPETITION

Purpose of the Chapter

Pure competition is the model that best illustrates price theory and its techniques. It also has some bearing on the real world. An understanding of the theoretical models here can aid in general comprehension of the pricing process in a dynamic economy.

Areas for Special Attention

1. Easy entry (and easy—if painful—exit) is a key to pure competition.
2. The "competition" of pure competition is highly impersonal, both as it affects buyers and sellers.
3. Pure competition illustrates the point about high prices stimulating production. After production has gone up, the prices fall back down.

Topics for Class Discussion

1. How important is factor mobility in pure competition?
2. Would the profitless long-run equilibrium have to cover all costs? (Note: Yes. This includes opportunity costs; thus economic "no profit" might be consistent with some recorded accounting profit.)
3. Would firms enter a profitable field if they knew profits would be wiped out? (Note: Probably they would, assuming nothing better was available.)

True-False Questions

T 1. Higher egg prices would encourage people to enter poultry farming.
T 2. Adam Smith thought rising prices would encourage entry of firms into an industry.
F 3. Perfect information is needed in pure competition.
F 4. Most firms in pure competition regard other firms as rivals for acceptance in the market.
T 5. The number of firms needed in pure competition is defined as "many."
T 6. The industry supply in the market period is the horizontal summation of the firms' supply curves.

F 7. Current production cost determines the supply curve in the market period.

F 8. The cost of new plant and equipment influences the short-run price.

T 9. Price must be above AVC in the short run if the firm is to produce.

F 10. In pure competition, profits can be made in the long run by keeping competitors out.

Suggested Answers for Questions at the End of the Chapter

1. It is the market structure in which many firms sell a standardized product.
2. It shows something of some real world markets, and it gives insights into the mechanics of the pricing process.
3. The incentive of a high enough price to give hope of profit.
4. Sellers need information to plan production and plant construction. The business press, regular newspapers, trade associations, and government all furnish information on current prices. They also give forecasts on which estimates of the future can be based.
5. Factors do not move into new profitable fields because of unwillingness, lack of money to support a move, and fear of a new situation.
6. Non-price competition covers quality, styling, service, etc. It is very important in many fields. It may, however, allow some prices to stay above the low levels which would enable the maximizing of consumer satisfaction.
7. The period too short to permit new production to take place.
8. Price and marginal cost.
9. It will go up, since some firms will leave the industry (reducing supply).
10. It could bring about lower prices in some fields. The main drawbacks would be the boredom of homogeneous products and the possible inefficiencies of the "many" necessarily small firms.)

CHAPTER 16

PROBLEMS OF COMPETITION

Purpose of the Chapter

The theoretical model of competition possesses many advantages (chiefly efficiency in allocating the resources in accordance with

37

demand). This chapter presents some of the problems that have plagued real world producers in highly competitive fields. It also demonstrates the point that industries troubled by competition often seek some form of government aid.

Areas for Special Attention

The industries discussed in the chapter are not necessarily perfect examples of pure competition. They seem, however, to represent fields in which the model does have some applicability.

A reference for this chapter and for Chapter 19 is <u>Public Policies Toward Business</u> by Clair Wilcox (Richard D. Irwin, Homewood, Ill., 1960).

Topics for Class Discussion

1. What is so good about competition and productivity increases? They have not brought much satisfaction to those in agriculture.
2. What goals should we be seeking in farm policy over the next ten years?
3. There is perennial pressure for a Federal Resale Price Maintenance law. Should this be enacted?

True-False Questions

T   1. From 1949 to 1961 there was a 15 per cent decline in the number of acres harvested.

F   2. People eat more wheat per capita now then they did in 1900, as a result of our increase in income.

F   3. Price-support programs give most benefit to the smallest farmers.

F   4. Purchases of products by the Commodity Credit Corporation reduce the total demand for the product.

T   5. Acreage allotments reduce supply.

T   6. The Soil Bank program calls for voluntary retirement of land.

F   7. The 1910-1914 base period for the parity index was dropped in 1939.

F   8. Automobile manufacturing is a "sick industry."

T   9. "Gray" cotton cloth is a standardized commodity.

T 10. Since 1953 the resale price maintenance laws of sixteen states have been nullified by the courts of the states.

Suggested Answers for Questions at the End of the Chapter

1. Ease of entry encourages active competition. Certainly with easy entry the price cannot long remain much above the cost of production, as it can with difficult entry.

2. Because of improved labor and management (better education), better capital equipment (tractors and other machines), and better seed and fertilizer. These have in some cases been encouraged by the state and Federal governments.

3. The demand per capita has gone down as tastes have shifted to foods like meat, fruits, and vegetables. This shift has been permitted by rising incomes.

4. One is to preserve the farm-family way of life. Another is to retain the political support of farm states; these have two United States Senators each, even with low total population.

5. It is the Federal agency that buys surplus crops in order to raise the price.

6. It can raise demand (by buying for itself). It can reduce supply. The second is cheaper unless large payments are used to encourage retirement of land. Compulsory allotments are the cheapest method.

7. It is the voluntary program, started in 1956, that pays farmers to retire part of their land. It is designed to reduce total output and conserve the soil. It often fails in the first objective, if remaining land can make up for the output lost in the retired land.

8. Parity relates change in prices farmers pay to changes in prices farmers receive. If both groups triple, farmers still are in the same relative position. Since 1910-1914, however, prices received have generally gone up more slowly than prices paid. (Thus the index usually has shown less than 100 per cent of parity.) Perhaps the main weaknesses of the concept are these:

   (a) A valid price index over a long period is hard to construct.

   (b) Productivity increases in agriculture are above average, but this fact is ignored. High productivity makes possible rising incomes, even without rising prices. In short, quantity as well as price should be considered.

9. Large ones benefit most. Price-support programs obviously do little good for those with little to sell. Large farmers have been known to get benefits worth $100,000 per year from the Federal programs.

10. For: They help protect small businessmen from large price-cutting competitors. They protect the prestige of manufacturers' brands; such prestige can be hurt by cutting the items' price.

   Against: They protect inefficient firms from competition. They discourage innovations that would lead to lower-cost marketing. They lower consumers' standards of living

39

PART VI. THE MONOPOLISTIC AND IMPERFECTLY COMPETITIVE FIRM

CHAPTER 17

MONOPOLY

Purpose of the Chapter

This chapter presents the theory of monopoly price. It also discusses the principles of regulation of prices charged by public utility monopolies.

Areas for Special Attention

Students often fail to grasp that the intersection of MC and MR is the profit-maximizing quantity. To sell this quantity, the monopolist finds the price on the demand curve that lies on the quantity. The charging of the profit-maximizing price leads to the selling of the profit-maximizing quantity.

Topics for Class Discussion

1. Is the current seventeen-year basic patent period too long? (Senator Estes Kefauver once suggested a three-year period as preserving incentives yet permitting more competition.)
2. If a monopolist has imperfect knowledge of his costs, is he more likely to guess at a price above or one below the profit-maximizing price?
3. Should prices of optional extra items (like the Bell System's "Princess" telephone) be subject to regulation? (Note: Currently they are, but apparently commissions accept the firm's suggested prices.)

True-False Questions

<u>T</u> 1. Patents grant monopolies to their holders.
<u>F</u> 2. Before 1911 the Standard Oil monopoly was based on control of raw materials.
<u>F</u> 3. Competition is always more efficient than monopoly.
<u>T</u> 4. The monopolist must know his costs, if he is to maximize his profits.

F 5. Marginal revenue is the profit gained from a smaller division within a large firm.

F 6. The monopolist sets his own demand curve, unlike the demand curve for the product in competition.

T 7. The monopolist should produce the quantity where MC cuts MR, if he wants to maximize profits.

T 8. Profit equals total revenue less total cost.

F 9. The Federal government handles all public utility regulations in the United States.

T 10. In a period of inflation, public utilities prefer valuation based on replacement value rather than historical cost.

Suggested Answers for Questions at the End of the Chapter

1. Control of raw materials, patents, and predatory practices are mentioned in the text. Superior performance in the market could perhaps be added, as could franchise grants by governments.

2. Fields where competition—even one other firm—would increase costs drastically. The public utilities are leading examples.

3. The addition to total revenue caused by the sale of one more unit.

4. He produces the quantity at which marginal cost cuts up through marginal revenue, and he charges the price that lies above this point on the demand curve.

5. An excessively high price lowers profits. Perhaps it is a characteristic of monopolists that they are slow to experiment and that they fear that demand is inelastic. If it is highly elastic, a price cut may well raise profits.

6. The purely competitive firm produces up to the point at which marginal cost equals price (which is the firm's demand curve). In the long run this is at the bottom of AC. The monopolist cuts production off short of this point to maximize profits. In so doing he holds price above AC. (Relate this to Figure 17.1.)

7. It can lead to wide variations in possible choices of a rate base. It also gives the well-prepared representatives of utilities an opportunity to bargain advantageously.

8. To reach a balance between high and low rates that permits moderate prices for consumers and yet sufficient returns to the utilities to encourage them to provide adequate (and improving) service.

CHAPTER 18

IMPERFECT COMPETITION

Purpose of the Chapter

The intermediate market structures of monopolistic competition and oligopoly form the subject matter of this chapter. The features of these market structures are emphasized. In addition, some of the practical problems of pricing in imperfect competition receive attention.

Areas for Special Attention

All of the market structures may be defined in terms of two variables—number of firms (many, few, or one) and nature of the product (differentiated or homogeneous). A review of these variables will help students to fit monopolistic competition and oligopoly into the whole pattern.

Pure competition and pure monopoly have the advantage of analytical precision. The two imperfectly competitive markets can be presented graphically, but perhaps emphasis is better placed on the uncertainties of the real world and on the necessity of using judgment and even educated guesses.

Topics for Class Discussion

1. In what sense is monopolistic competition "monopolistic" and in what sense is it "competitive"?
2. What accounts for the "fewness" of firms in oligopoly?
3. Why might a firm choose a low ("penetration") price for a new item or a high ("cream-skimming") price?

True-False Questions

F 1. In monopolistic competition the product can be either homogeneous or differentiated.
T 2. Store location can affect price.
T 3. There is easy entry into monopolistic competition.
T 4. In oligopoly the product can be either differentiated or homogeneous.
F 5. The price leader is the firm that can initiate an industry price cut.
F 6. Price leadership has not been observed in the United States economy since World War II.

F 7. High entry costs are a characteristic of monopolistic competition.

T 8. Oligopolists have greater choice in pricing than profit-maximizing pure monopolists.

F 9. Fixed costs are ignored in setting up a break-even chart.

T 10. Expected sales volume must be known to set price by the target rate of return method.

Suggested Answers for Questions at the End of the Chapter

1. Monopolistic competition involves product differentiation; pure competition requires a homogeneous product.
2. Relatively elastic. A small price increase would cause great loss of sales to other firms.
3. In the long run, pure competitors produce at the bottom of the AC curve. In monopolistic competition, price would probably remain above this low level, but volume would be less too, because of excessive entry. Thus monopolistic competition would use more resources and still charge a higher price (without high profits).
4. It is stronger where products are homogeneous. Here price cuts must always be matched, since differentiated oligopolists might still make sales at a higher price on the basis of non-price advantages.
5. The price leader is the firm that can raise price and be followed. Because of dominant market position or good market understanding, this firm's increase is thought to be one which will allow all firms to increase profits by raising price.
6. High cost of entry and the great market acceptance attained by established firms. Perhaps it would cost close to a billion dollars to start a major automobile firm in the United States. Even then it would be very hard to sell cars because of the strength of consumer preferences for established makes.
7. Prices set by managerial judgment in the imperfectly competitive markets in which costs and demand are not known with absolute certainty.
8. It would need to know or estimate its fixed cost, the pattern of variable costs over the output range, and the sales volume at each of the prices under consideration.
9. The market strength of the firm is the basic determinant, that is, the nature of the demand curve facing the firm. Implicit in this analysis is the assumption that the firm could charge a higher price and reap higher profits. Thus it has a strong market position and perhaps even inelastic demands. It does not, however, exploit this fact to maximize short-run profits. Perhaps it seeks to retain public goodwill and maximize long-range profits.

CHAPTER 19

PROBLEMS OF MONOPOLY AND IMPERFECT COMPETITION

Purpose of the Chapter

This chapter presents a discussion of the laws that prevent non-purely competitive firms from charging excessively high prices and harming both the competitive system and competitors themselves.

Areas for Special Attention

The antitrust laws were developed over a long period. Those discussed here emphasize the activities of larger firms to suppress competition. Recall, however, that in Chapter 16 it was shown that some laws (such as Resale Price Maintenance) encourage the suppression of competition. It is also possible that the Robinson-Patman Act suppresses as much competition as it encourages

One key to this confusion is the thought that the whole pattern of laws seeks to encourage the existence of many competitors. Thus much of the emphasis is on sellers, rather than on consumers and the benefits they might get from more active price competition among somewhat fewer competitors. It can always be argued that elimination of small competitors would lead ultimately to less competition between the remaining giants.

Topics for Class Discussion

1. Which antitrust law is most important to consumers?
2. Compare Section Two of the Sherman Act with Section Two of the Clayton Act (as amended).
3. Should antitrust enforcement be more or less vigorous? (Note: Emphasize what economic goals you value.)

True-False Questions

T 1. Before 1890, stockholders of competing firms sometimes let a single board of trustees vote all their stock.

T 2. Price-fixing agreements are illegal under Section One of the Sherman Act.

F 3. Price-fixing involves only money penalties.

F 4. The last firm to be actually broken up was the Standard Oil Company in 1945.

F   5. The rule of reason was originated in the Alcoa case.
T   6. The Morton Salt case was brought under the Robinson-Patman Act.
T   7. The Robinson-Patman Act allows lower prices for some customers if they are fully justified by savings in cost.
F   8. The Celler-Kefauver Act prohibits "tying contracts."
F   9. A person can serve on the board of directors of two large competing firms if the FTC approves it.
T 10. The Wheller-Lea Act amended the FTC Act.

Suggested Answers for Questions at the End of the Chapter

1. It stimulates managerial initiative, encourages efficiency, and lowers prices.
2. A board of trustees voted the stock of all firms in an industry. Thus the industry operated as a monopolized whole, rather than as a group of competing firms.
3. It prohibits agreements among competitors (Section One) and also monopolies and attempts to monopolize (Section Two).
4. The rule from the 1911 Standard Oil case that only "reasonable" monopolies should be broken up.
5. The Division concentrates on the Sherman Act; it is closely associated with the current administration. The FTC is a body independent of the current administration; it emphasizes the Clayton Act and has exclusive jurisdiction over the FTC Act.
6. It prevents large buyers (such as chains) from getting low buying prices that they could get on the basis of their market power. These low prices would presumably be passed on to consumers; in the process, however, smaller competitors would lose their customers.
7. Contracts in which an unwanted item must be bought in order for the buyer to get a wanted item. In one case a major film producer was ordered to "untie" the development service from the sale of the film itself. Formerly the film and its processing had been a "package deal" (allegedly depriving independent processors from getting a change at the processing business).
8. It prohibits mergers that might lessen the number of separate competitors.
9. The FTC has the authority to issue "cease and desist" orders against misleading advertisements.
10. In some fields there may be, although specific facts are not known. Some bigness is needed for peak efficiency, but if this causes excessive fewness of competitors, the benefits of the efficiency to consumers may be lost.

PART VII. THE DISTRIBUTION OF INCOME

CHAPTER 20

WAGES: LABOR'S INCOME SHARE

Purpose of the Chapter

This chapter considers the theory of wage determination. It includes discussion of union effect on wages and considers the minimum wage legislation.

Areas for Special Attention

1. The statement that wages should be related to productivity is often heard. The marginal revenue product gives a precise foundation for this statement.
2. The union-wage relationship is one for which snap judgments should be avoided. Similarly the <u>exact</u> results of minimum wage laws are elusive.

Topics for Class Discussion

1. Can higher wages stimulate productivity?
2. Should there be a minimum wage high enough to secure a decent standard of living for all workers?
3. Do unions really have the power to set wages above the market level?

True-False Questions

F   1. Labor usually gets about half of the national income.

F   2. Economists agree that higher wages would substantially raise the size of the labor force.

T   3. If workers are immobile, the labor supply curve is probably inelastic.

F   4. The small firm in a large labor market must raise wages, if it is to get additional workers.

T   5. The marginal revenue product is the same as a demand curve.

T   6. Under the 1938 Fair Labor Standards Act the minimum wage was 25 cents per hour.

<u>F</u> 7. The Minimum Wage Act covers only the first forty hours of work per week.
<u>T</u> 8. Workers displaced by a minimum wage law can seek employment in a "uncovered" industry.
<u>F</u> 9. Wages seldom increase in nonunion plants.
<u>T</u> 10. Current money wages can increase faster than productivity.

Suggested Answers for Questions at the End of the Chapter

1. About two-thirds. Stable.
2. On balance they have little effect. High wages encourage some to work, but permit others (women and young people) to quit. Low wages may discourage some from working, but they may force others (those women and young people again) into the labor force.
3. Immobility makes supply inelastic, especially as it is seen by a firm.
4. Productivity as measured by the marginal revenue product.
5. The addition to the value of production caused by the addition of an extra worker. (The concept can be applied to other productive factors, too.)
6. Besides raising some wages and lowering profits it can do these things:
    Stimulate a price increase
    Stimulate a productivity increase
    Drive employers out of business
    Cause workers to lose jobs
    Lower wages in "uncovered" field
7. It can happen if the lowest-skilled workers crowd into the uncovered fields after losing their jobs in covered fields (assuming they cannot be made to be "worth" the minimum wage).
8. Perhaps they do, but wages go up in nonunion fields too. Also it could be argued that unions have sought out the most productive fields for organizing. Probably a union's biggest real increase occurs when it first comes in; after that it tends to be limited by routine productivity increases.
9. Economists argue both ways. Perhaps large unions push for increases over productivity, confident that government will stimulate demand enough to prevent unemployment. This is hard to prove, however, and it still rests on the volume of aggregate demand. Since aggregate demand is the key, and since we have had considerable unemployment, the macroeconomic explanation seems preferable.

CHAPTER 21

INTEREST, RENTS, AND PROFITS:
OTHER FACTORS INCOME SHARES

Purpose of the Chapter

In this chapter the determination of other factors of production income is considered. The application of economic theory is attempted.

Areas for Special Attention

1. The relationship among interest-rate determination and the size of investment and the problem of the gold outflow can be reviewed here.
2. Rent theory is one of the oldest areas of economic thought. This reflects the basic nature of land.
3. There is a question as to whether profit is like other factor returns. It may be handled as such without great problems.

Topics for Class Discussion

1. Do expensive rents force stores in high-rent districts to charge high prices or does the chance to get high prices cause store opperators to bid up rents?
3. Which is more important, the expectation of profit or the actual getting of profit?

True-False Questions

F 1. Total rent income is larger than total interest income.
T 2. The supply of loanable funds is determined mainly by the Federal Reserve.
T 3. An increase in the demand for loanable funds raises the interest rate, other things equal.
F 4. American interest rates lower than those abroad help attract gold to the United States.
F 5. A recession usually lowers interest rates.
F 6. Henry George advocated the raising of rents.
T 7. The level of rents is determined mainly by the influence of demand on a scarce item.
F 8. John Maynard Keynes was chiefly interested in profit theory.

<u>F</u> 9. The major continuing source of profits for most firms is windfalls.

<u>T</u> 10. Fads are short-lived innovations.

Suggested Answers for Questions at the End of the Chapter

1. It influences the supply of money (see Chapter 7). A larger money supply lowers interest, other things equal. Such an increase can come from the Fed's buying government bonds on the open market.
2. The demand of business firms to borrow to buy merchandise, materials, plant, and equipment; the demand of consumers to borrow for homes, durable goods, etc.; and the demand for borrowed funds of government.
3. Higher interest rates discourage borrowers; only the most essential or most profitable projects are undertaken if rates are high.
4. Low rates encourage investment and other spending, but higher rates keep foreign money attracted in this country and lessen the gold outflow.
5. It tends to be inelastic. The amount of land is relatively fixed.
6. He advocated a single tax which would be all the rental value of land. He claimed that society should have this amount, since society created this value.
7. Opportunity cost should be deducted from reported profit to get true economic profit. Proprietor's wage value and interest not earned on money invested in the business are example.
8. New products and processes raise profits. Nylon for Du Pont, automatic transmissions for General Motors, and dial telephones for the Bell Systems are illustrations.

CHAPTER 22

TAXES: GOVERNMENT'S INCOME SHARE

Purpose of the Chapter

This chapter presents some of the basic concepts that underlie our tax system. It also introduces the major taxes, emphasizing their mechanics and considering some current issues associated with them. The whole taxing and spending pattern, Federal, state, and local is also explored.

Areas for Special Attention

1. The fact that state and local taxes, considered as a whole, are regressive is often ignored. This would seem to call for a progressive Federal system of taxes, even if strict proportionality were sought.
2. Modern fiscal policy employs tax changes as a basic tool. Check the current tax laws; the Internal Revenue Service is generous with booklets and poster-size editions of the major tax forms (such as the 1040) for classroom use. Another excellent source is <u>Financing Government</u> by Harold M. Groves (Holt, Rinehart and Winston, New York, 1964).

Topics for Class Discussion

1. Should the tax system be more progressive?
2. Which taxes are most "painless" to taxpayers?
3. If government spending were increased to an extent requiring higher tax rates, which taxes should be raised?

True-False Questions

F 1. Taxes take over half of our national income.

T 2. The gasoline tax can be justified under the benefits-received principle.

T 3. For a progressive tax, the percentage rate goes up as the base goes up.

F 4. The cigarette tax is progressive.

F 5. The tax on corporation profits is the largest revenue producer of the Federal government.

T 6. If a taxpayer has more withheld than the final amount of his tax, he can apply for a refund.

F 7. The only way benefits can be collected under Social Security is for the taxpayer to live to retirement age.

T 8. National defense is the largest category of Federal spending.

T 9. Business property taxes are the largest revenue producer in the state and local government groups.

F 10. The personal exemption was raised from $600 to $1,000 in 1964.

Suggested Answers for Questions at the End of the Chapter

1. Many have a benefits-received aspect. Among them are the property tax, the gasoline tax, and the Social Security tax.
2. In proportional taxes, the percentage rate stays constant as the

base increases. In progressive taxes, the percentage rate increases as the base increases. In regressive taxes, the percentage rate decreases as the base increases.

3. It is regressive with respect to personal incomes rather than with respect to items taxed. Low-income persons spend more of their incomes on taxable items than wealthy persons, who save more and spend more on such things as stocks and bonds and trips abroad.

4. See Tables 22.2 and 22.3.

5. See Tables 22.4 and 22.5.

6. It is spending in specified categories (such as charitable contributions) which is deducted from gross income and is thus not included in taxable income. Other deductions include state and local taxes paid and interest paid.

7. The taxpayer gets some of his income in something other than current money wages. He then holds the item for the required holding period (six months, prior to 1964). If he later sells the item for more than the value at time of acquisition, the gain is subject only to the lower capital gains rate.

8. They are stated percentages of gross income which a firm can deduct; thus they make taxable income lower. Such allowances are given to firms in industries using up natural resources. The $27\frac{1}{2}$ per cent depletion allowance in the oil industry is the largest and best known (and most controversial).

9. Among possibilities are these: change depletion allowances, change the items allowed as deductions in personal income taxes, raise, or lower the personal exemption, and withhold taxes from dividends on corporation stock.

10. Check with the Internal Revenue Service for this information. Often the local post office will have some of the IRS information in brief booklet form.

PART VIII. CONCLUSIONS

CHAPTER 23

ECONOMIC PROBLEMS: PAST, PRESENT, FUTURE

Purpose of the Chapter

This chapter is designed to review the whole subject of economics. It attempts to present a full view of the subject, both in its current dimensions and in historical perspective.

Areas for Special Attention

At this point a pulling together of ideas and a general synthesizing is desirable.

Topics for Class Discussion

1. What truly "modern" economic problems are there?
2. Contrast Adam Smith and John Maynard Keynes with respect to their policy views.
3. How do competing goals make the solution of economic problems more difficult? (Note: Full employment may make price stability harder to achieve, low versus high interest rates, bigness in business for efficiency versus competition.)

True-False Questions

F   1. Adam Smith emphasized the need for government policies to bring full employment.

T   2. Jevons was a pioneer in the study of the business cycle.

T   3. In 1963, unemployment of teen-agers was over twice the overall national rate.

T   4. The price index of wholesale industrial commodities did not go up during the 1961-1963 period.

F   5. The $1 Federal Reserve Notes were issued because of the gold outflow.

F   6. An increase in portfolio investments abroad can help solve the balance-of-payments problem.

F   7. The Celler-Kefauver Act of 1950 prevents the growth of large firms through internal expansion.

T 8. Skilled jobs are growing in number faster than unskilled jobs.

F 9. Macroeconomic theory cannot be used by a firm in forecasting.

T 10. It is possible for a firm to find out something about its product's demand elasticity through economic research.

Suggested Answers for Questions at the End of the Chapter

1. We assume that it is the nature of man always to want more than he has.
2. Smith's work was encyclopedic, but perhaps it is a fair summary to state that he emphasized the value of allowing the price system to be the basic regulator of the economy. In this way consumer demand would be supplied through profit incentives of producers.
3. In the "iron law of wages," Ricardo extended Malthus' concepts of population growth pressures into a theory of wage determination (at the subsistence level).
4. Keynes stated that flexible prices and an adequate money supply were not alone adequate to ensure full employment.
5. In view of the compromise currently required, we should seek a low enough level to encourage investment (assuming inflation is not a problem), while maintaining a high enough level to keep money from being attracted out of the country.
6. This is a debatable point. It is likely that the field is large enough for both. A recent estimate by a Labor Department spokesman said that 70,000 jobs per week would have to be provided during the rest of the 1960s just to keep up with new workers and new technology. It is the author's opinion that business will take on the training job most eagerly during a period of high-level full employment when there is really something approaching a labor shortage. If government can produce this condition, then the private sector can be expected to provide the training.
7. Raising growth adds permanently billions of dollars per year to the GNP. Lowering prices would benefit far fewer people (creditors, those on fixed income). In addition, it is hard to picture a means of lowering prices that would not involve a general depressant effect on the economy.
8. They replaced silver certificates which were retired to make silver sales by the Treasury possible. This in turn was to keep the silver price down to $1.29. If the price went greatly above this, a melting down of small silver change could occur, and this would hamper normal business.

9. They involve an outflow of money from the United States. Further, they have little benefit to this country. Because of this, such investment has been discouraged (through the threat of a tax) in order to help us approach balance-of-payments equilibrium at a "favorable" level.

10. Merger growth is the subject of much current antitrust policy. Under Celler-Kefauver many mergers can be halted. Firms that merged in the past, however, and are now growing greatly through reinvesting profits (such as General Motors) cannot be touched under this law. These firms might eventually be adjudged monopolies under this law. These firms might eventually be adjudged monopolies under Section Two of the Sherman Act, but such cases are hard for the government to win in the absence of a pure monopoly.

11. Forecasting of the level of macroeconomic activity and analysis of demand and costs would rank near the top.